Strands of Rhyme:
POEMS FROM THE REAL WORLD

RITA FIDLER DORN

To order additional copies of this book, contact:
Xlibris LLC
1-888-795-4274
www.Xlibris.com
Orders@Xlibris.com
542728

WHAT ARE PEOPLE SAYING ABOUT *STRANDS OF RHYME*?

"Rita is a most talented writer with a true gift for expression. Her poetry reflects her life's journey, some steps of which she shares with her readers."
Shelley Engle, *social services practitioner*

"Her work resounds with the laughter and tears we have all experienced."
Rabbi/Cantor Danny Marmorstein, *spiritual leader*

"I love her poems. They are simple, yet deep and full of truth. They are smart and sensitive, and will definitely put a smile on your face."
Isabela S. Nobell, *artist, design entrepreneur*

"Let me be specific:
this book is terrific.
Dorn's work is really first rate.
I cannot raise
more prolific praise
than to say her book is just great !"
Alan Gardner, *insurance executive, poet*

"In this book, she gives us a lifetime of poems. Some are light, while others are quite deep. Each reflects her love of poetry, humanity, and rhyme."
Connie Goodman-Milone, M.S.W.,*writer*

"Her works are gourmet dishes from the heart, each flavored with her own unique life spices—those of wife, mother, grandmother, professor, poet, and friend."
Elizabeth R. Stockton, *certified neurologic music therapist*

LET THESE STRANDS WRAP THEMSELVES AROUND YOU.

"Prepare to be bewitched . . . . when you read Ricki's poems. A wizard of words, lyrical verse, meter, and rhyme. A poet who vividly paints images, experiences, human emotions, humor, and beauty of nature. Her creativity captures your imagination and turns ordinary to profound. Every page in this book is her canvas; the pen is her brush; words describing feelings and stories are her paint. Result? A masterpiece!"

Evelyn Benson, *grant writer, former editor of* Florida Foreign Trade Review

"One word, wonderful!"

Dorothy Danaher White, **Ph.D,** *psychologist, playwright*

"Ricki is a smiling, caring person who loves words and people, all evident in her poetry. Her descriptions stir emotions and her workshops are awesome. Students lucky enough to be in her classes are in for a treat, as she is a both a creative writer and well-versed in grammar."

Cara Nusinov, *certified poetry therapist, artist*

"I knew Ricki before, during, and since her tenure as president of South Florida Writers Association. One thing stands out: her passion for poetry. You will see this in her book."

Jonathan Rose, *attorney, writer, cultural correspondent*

TABLE OF CONTENTS

CITIES and OTHER PLACES

CONFLICT

LOVE, ETC.

REMEMBERING

SEASONS, TIME, and WEATHER

SELVES

WORDS ON WORDS

FOREWORD

I first met Rita Dorn in the spring of 2007. As a new Miami resident and college student, I was welcomed by Rita and her husband Jeff to a city where I had no family or friends. I soon learned of Rita's love for literature, particularly her passion for poetry. I became so encouraged by her that I began to read and write poetry myself again; I even dug up poems I had written in high school to share with her. What inspired me, too, was her admiration for two of her favorites, Emily Dickinson and Robert Frost. This led to my own participation in several workshops and numerous poetry readings over the following few years.

It has been my pleasure and privilege to enjoy many of the poems in this book. Her poetry is both daring and vulnerable, witty yet heartfelt, and deeply personal while very relatable to the reader. This collection is sure to inspire whoever reads it. It is my honor to call Rita my friend, and I'm happy that everyone can now enjoy her published words.

Anthony Torres, Jr.,
Psychology Doctoral Candidate

ACKNOWLEDGMENTS

Gratitude goes to my husband, Jeffrey, for being another pair of eyes, always perceptive. To my son, Tobin, for generously and skillfully creating the perfect cover art for this book. To my son, Corey, for his astute organizational ideas. To my dear friend, Barbara Blitfield Pech, for being my Brooklyn consultant. To my talented writing colleague, Gonny van den Broek, for her valuable editing skills. To novelist Bethe Moulton for her wise counsel on publishing issues. To The South Florida Writers Association for being a wellspring of encouragement. And to all of my friends, enemies, relatives, and strangers whose paths have crossed mine, contributing to my rich myriad of life experiences.

INTRODUCTION

Dear Reader,

This project has been a work in progress since I was about ten years old. I vowed that when I grew up, I would write a book of poetry, entitled *Rainbeams,* referring to the damp sorrows and sunny joys in life. The title evolved to *Strands of Rhyme,* but I kept all the poems I wrote in those intervening years, transferring them from backs of envelopes, sheets of notebook paper, and wrinkled cocktail napkins to first the typewriter and later the computer. This book is a selection from that vast storehouse.

My purpose in writing poetry is to respond to what happens in the world, as well as to what happens to me and to other people. Furthermore, it is to share my words with others, and to tweak the quiet little poet who is perhaps hiding inside of you, my reader. If you find some poems in this book to which you can really relate, which make you think, feel, smile, and connect, then my mission will have been accomplished. Good reading (and maybe good writing).

R.F.D.

DEDICATION

This book is warmly dedicated to my sons, Tobin and Corey, with all my love and affection.

This book is lovingly dedicated to my husband, Jeffrey, who has been my mirror, my muse, and my motivator for much of what I have accomplished in my adult life. His optimism and humor have brightened up my sometimes dark outlooks. He has been the shelter from my many storms; he is and always will be my best friend.

IN MEMORY

In cherished memory of my parents, Beatrice and David Fidler, and my brother, Eric Stephan Fidler, all of whose loving thumbprints I still carry with me today.

SOCIAL COMMENTARY

"Feelings of worth can flourish only in an atmosphere where individual differences are appreciated, mistakes are tolerated, communication is open, and rules are flexible . . . ."
—Virginia Satir

"Moral certainty is always a sign of cultural inferiority. The more uncivilized the man, the surer he is that he knows precisely what is right and what is wrong. All human progress . . . . has been the work of men who have doubted the current moral values, not of men who have whooped them up and tried to enforce them. The truly civilized man is always skeptical and tolerant."
— H.L. Mencken

CHANGE

Change
frightens us, worries us,
disrupts us, assaults us,
shoots terror of the unknown
into our couch-potato hearts.

Change
motivates us, thrills us, impels us,
offers fresh opportunity to grow and achieve,
places a ticket to uncharted territory
in our sweaty hands.

Change
envelopes the present,
becomes the old,
is replaced by newer change.

Should be embraced as an ally;
if viewed as a foe, it will emerge victorious.

1996

BODY PIERCER-IN-RESIDENCE

Bag boy, construction, take-out cook--
some of our son's jobs while in college,
but the winner was the one he learned
on his own, with self-acquired knowledge.

> Certain friends had jewelry on their skin;
> our son deemed them cool, and mused how to begin;
> he got a few piercings, watched how they were done,
> and asked his dad to be Client Number One.

To show support, his dad tensely agreed,
and happily lived to tell the tale;
even tried to interest some of his own friends,
but that was to no avail.

> Our son pierced a few pals, as favors, for free;
> his skill and confidence grew, we could see.
> His shop: my dining table, our sofa: the waiting room;
> he had cards printed, and business began to boom.

He did tongues and belly buttons for some,
eyebrows, *labrets*, and noses for others;
customers came with their boyfriends or girlfriends;
a few even arrived with their mothers.

> I stocked our freezer with Baggies of ice cubes
> to numb soreness and keep the swelling down;
> he was clean, cute, honest, and funny;
> his good reputation spread all over town.

One girl showed up with her father, a doctor,
who brought a syringe of Xylocaine
hoping to spare his child discomfort;
but she said, "No problem, Daddy, no pain."

> Our son pored over jewelry magazines
> and learned quickly which styles would sell;
> he constantly honed his technique.
> In this profession, he did quite well.

Our son earned enough money that year
to go to Europe and buy himself a truck;
he credits his success to hard work, ethics,
passion for his craft, and, of course, some luck.
       Widespread demand for piercing fell somewhat,
       and like all bubbles do, one day, this one burst;
       but of the stories he'll tell his own teens some day,
       this colorful episode may be one of the first.

FEELINGS OF FRIENDSHIP

Being with old friends

is like wearing a soft, sweet, well-washed pair of jeans . . .
warm, enveloping, and comfy; you know they will always fit.

It's not being able to do or say anything wrong.
Those treasured friends love your jokes, keep your secrets,
and take no offense at your constructive little criticisms.

It's like being in your childhood home, if that was a good place,
where you felt secure and accepted, where no harm could reach you.

Old friends are heirlooms which you never want to be without.
They are in you, with you, part of your operating system,
past and present. The mirrors of your years.

Finding new friends

is like wearing an evening gown for the first time or
donning a crisp, fresh tuxedo shirt. They offer the thrill of a
ride on a Harley on a windy hill, surprises every few minutes.

It's navigating uncharted territory, poised for new discoveries at any
moment. They offer the delight of discovering shared connections.

New friends are like starting a book whose pages tempt you with
adventures to come. They are like the first day of school.
Making new friends is like standing at the foot of a mountain,
looking up and imagining the thrills that await you above.

> If old friends are the staples you cannot do without,
> then new friends are the spices you don't want to miss.

2006

RITA FIDLER DORN

AND I NEVER THOUGHT TO ASK

Since we left the condo,
warmly dressed and fully fed,
we wandered out into the day
but three vital things were left unsaid . . . .
and I never thought to ask.

We danced, sang, and skated
and kissed deeply in the rain,
but you never said you'd call me soon
or "Can I see you again?"
And I never thought to ask.

You shared your teenaged antics
and amusing childhood tales,
but you never said what we would do,
if our protection failed.
And I never thought to ask.

We ate and drank;
we laughed and tarried,
but you never told me
that you were married.
And I never thought to ask.

POOLSIDE

Feeling far too fat that day to wear a swimsuit,
but craving the wafting poolside breeze
and fresh, chlorine scent,
I wore a skimpy sun dress to the hotel pool deck
with bra and panties beneath it.

The tranquil swimming pool's only audience,
he and I sat several lounge chairs away from each other,
respite from the intense verbal, sexual, and emotional intimacy
of the past 24 hours,

Soon bored with the local newsprint and
a recently purchased poetry book,
I wandered over to the jacuzzi, which was
snugly positioned on the perimeter of the pool court.
Inhabited by a few lone twigs and antisocial insects,
the unpristine water beckoned me seductively. Briefly,
I thought of my rejected swimsuit back in the room.

Lowering my behind onto the dry second step,
and pushing my skirts back,
I let my toes, ankles, calves, knees, and upper thighs
be caressed by the tepid wetness of the lackadaisical water.
Slowly inching deeper into its modest depths,
I felt the water boldly advance and cooly, confidently, courageously,
rendezvous with the edge of my silk, flowered underpants.

2010

FROM THE KITCHENS OF POVERTY

From the kitchens of poverty,
through windows of indifference,
on the streets of violence:
they yearn to overcome.

Throughout the cities of rebellion,
amid the fields of prejudice,
within the valleys of ignorance:
they yearn to overcome.

In the pangs of hunger,
on the beds of sickness,
with the chill of homelessness:
they yearn to overcome.

From the pain of conflict
and the battlefields of blood,
to the task of rebuilding:
we all aspire to a world of peace.

2004

KIDS

Babies and toddlers, so cute, soft, and sweet . . .
when they smile and gurgle, your heart skips a beat.

You have all those goals for them, high hopes and bright dreams;
the best of life: the cherry, the nuts, the whipped cream.

Then they grow older and conflicts ensue;
you love them and care; what's a parent to do?

Daughter says, *"Your religion's a joke;"*
I won't live my life under that yoke."

Your son says, *"Dad, I should tell you, I'm gay.*
I don't care to have sex your way."

Your youngest says clearly, *"I'm going out to get high;*
anymore flack and I won't return. Good bye."

The other one says *"Education's not so hot;*
me finish college? No, I think not."

All the dreams, all the hopes you expected to share . . .
like smoke, they evaporated into thin air.

"I don't have to repay those student loans—
it's my business now; don't nag me; I'm grown."

"I have no time to return your calls;
I have places to go: gym, clubs, malls."

"I'm pregnant, Mom, but I won't marry the dad;
he's stupid and said something that made me mad!"

"With you, at your house, I don't want to eat food;
truthfully, mom, your cooking's not good."

RITA FIDLER DORN

"I don't ask about your day—your life's a bore;
I'm not interested in hearing anymore."

You expected to walk them down the aisle,
but they wanted their space and wed far away, on the Nile.

All the dreams, all the hopes you expected to share . . .
like smoke, they evaporated into thin air.

"Why should I write a thank you note?
don't stuff your values down my throat."

"Hello, this is Officer Ainsley at the county jail;
your teenager is here and needs you to post bail."

"I don't have to respect you; don't care if you hate me;
why are you so hard to get along with lately?"

'I haven't called you in over a week?
So what! I'm busy—I'm cool, not a geek."

"My childhood was a challenge, as I can recall,
a mountain of problems and I had them all!"

You don't know where you erred, but you did your best
to put values and love into your family's nest.

All those years of parenting, totally wasted . . .
a few lone moments of joy were all you tasted.

All the dreams, all the hopes you expected to share,
like smoke, they evaporated into thin air.

2006

LIGHT

In the beginning there was darkness,
but the spirit of God hovered over the darkness.

Then God created light,
and the Work of Creation was begun.

Light is the symbol of divinity and goodness.
Light is the symbol of law and justice.

It is the outward sign of the inner spark
within each one of us.

Light is the symbol of warmth and unity,
binding us together with others.

Light is the symbol of day,
the dawn of new beginnings.

Light is the symbol of remembrance.

Light is a bond,
illuminating the memory of those whose
light is now extinguished.

SIGHS FOR THE ROADS NOT TAKEN

When we sigh for the roads not taken, we forget the beauty of those that we walked and the reasons why we chose them.

The aging bachelor views the empty chair beside him in his well-appointed living room, filled with fine antiques. As he eyes the unfilled seat, he forgets the luxury cruises, the gourmet meals, the red Porsche, the gold Rolex, and the seasons of oven-hot sex with a smorgasbord of world class women. *He sighs for a partner.*

The gray-haired matron listens to her grand-daughter extol the virtues of her current beau. Granny recalls the blaze of the handsome rogue she did not marry in favor of the balding accountant, who carpooled the kids, helped in the house, was supportive through her menopause, and doesn't mind her wrinkles. *She sighs for romance.*

The successful executive recalls the pregnancy she sacrificed for her career, which couldn't be interrupted. From her tinted limousine window, she watches a young mom herd two squirming toddlers across a busy street. Memory blurs her custom-built mansion, her designer wardrobe, her freedom to travel, practice yoga, and patronize the arts. *She sighs for motherhood.*

The optimistic gambler scrambled up the ladder of success, trading one position for a better one, one girlfriend for a younger one, one house for a bigger one, one set of friends for a richer set—until the swaps became downgrades and the "sure deals" began to sputter. He now eyes his cousin's big pension and small house payment, forgetting that his cousin toiled many years at the same job and lived in that modest little house for a long time. *He sighs for security.*

Sigh for the roads not taken if we must, but don't forget the joys of those we did. Even if we later decide that we chose wrong, just remember why we chose the roads we took.

THE GIVENS

We think it's a given that we have a good job, earn enough money,
        make the right choices, and be happy.
We think it's a given that our marriage be lasting and true,
        that our spouse won't lie to us or cheat on us,
        that we can always talk to each other,
        overlook the little things and overcome the big ones.
We think it's a given that we have healthy children,
        who will love each other, love us as much as we love them,
        and give us the respect we worked so hard to earn.
We think it's a given that our children
        won't cheat, do drugs, or abuse alcohol,
        won't be cruel to others or animals,
        will drive safely and obey the law,
        will live by the moral values we taught them and we lived by.
We think it's a given that they will choose partners
        of their own faith, of their own race, and of the opposite gender.
We think it's a given that we live to see our children get married,
        participate in that milestone, and
        share a healthy adult relationship.
We think it's a given that we
        feel close to our daughters-in-law and sons-in-law,
        receive pleasure from the grandchildren,
        approve of how our children are raising them,
            tell them stories they want to hear,
            spend birthdays and holidays together
            and fun afternoons at the zoo.

***But** we don't always get the givens that we thought we would,*
>*even though we tried so hard and are entitled to them.*
And one day we realize that not only did we not get the givens in the past,
>*but we may not get the givens in the future either.*
But because we didn't get the givens we know we should have gotten,
>*we got something else:*
>>*a dose of reality,*
>>*a splash of acceptance,*
>>*a layer of bitterness,*
>>*and a potful of strength to cope with it all.*
It isn't right and it isn't OK and it probably can't be changed,
>but that's what we got . . . . not having gotten the givens.

Contest Award Winner
November 2012 South Florida Writers Association

FAILURE

Failure seeps into your pores,
up your spine,
down your arms and legs, and
lodges in your psyche.

       It scars your mind, your brain,
       and your ego like an
       unwelcome but persistent guest;
       it's rational and irrational.

It makes you feel bad about yourself, all over,
whether or not it was your fault, but
especially if it wasn't. It gives you a
bitter taste that can't be diluted or expelled.

       The shroud of failure darkens
       your life and your being.
       Failure, an insidious affliction;
       there should be a vaccine for it.

2012

AGE, AGES, and AGING

*"As we soar into the skies of our future, we take our
past with us, as carry-on luggage."*
—R.F. Dorn

"Age is important, only if you are wine or cheese."

ANOTHER JANUARY 1ST

Another year, another chance, another new beginning,
an unturned page, with unread words. Untasted delicacies,
unrevealed opportunities, unknown experiences,
still hidden joys and, certainly, yet invisible agonies.
They are all waiting for me in the year ahead, ready to jump out
on their prescribed days and hours, right on cue.

What control have I over these "futures"?
Only how I view them, approach them, manage them.
Only how skillful I am in bending them to my will,
and, of course, some of them will bend me to theirs.
Twelve months from today, these now "unseens"
will move from the chapter called Future to the one called History.

2011

EMPTY NEST

I wanted a rest
and yearned for the nest
finally to be empty.

For my two little fledglings
to leave our edgings
and begin to fly on their own.

Well, now it's done;
they're up, out, and gone
—and I don't like it.

I wait for the evening, my "fix" and my "upper,"
when they drop by with laundry or for some supper.

I treasure each phone call,
when they make it all,
and try not to betray my hunger

For the days and the years,
despite battles and tears,
when they were both home, and younger.

The empty nest
is not the best,
but must be bravely endured.

RITA FIDLER DORN

I should focus on pride
and try not to chide
myself—I've good memories stored.

The tide of time, with its tempo of change,
always, at first, feels achy and strange;
now my birds live in the world they'll roam.

Toward new heights they'll soar,
venture far and explore,
knowing they can always come home.

1996

FARMER

Farmer, tarry not too long
in the field where you sow,
for the sun will have fallen
before you know.
Yes, the more you sow,
the more to reap,
but taste all the crops
before you sleep.

The sun's now high,
and the moon will glow;
don't let your fields
be all that you know.

1977

Rita Fidler Dorn

FRAGILE! HANDLE WITH CARE

One minute running to make a touchdown,
the next one lying motionless on the field.

One minute singing in the choir,
the next hour silent in a hospital bed.

One minute speeding down the highway to a party,
the next one speeding down the highway in an ambulance.

One minute cooking a tantalizing dinner,
the next one, lying on the floor, with empty hands.

One minute laughing so hard it hurts,
the next minute it only hurts.

One minute, the days ahead seem limitless;
the next one, the days are numbered.

Life is fragile: treat it gently, every minute.
It's fragile.

My Past Seems to Follow Me

My past seems to follow me,
      all of my life;
my girlhood casts shadows,
      'tho I'm now mother and wife.
I meet friends from high school
      wherever I go;
old beaux from college
      turn up, don't you know?
Even my ex-husband called up
      to have lunch,
but his goals weren't mine,
      I have a hunch.

What can I do? Will I never be free
      of previous people who happened to me?

Of lives that I led
      in earlier places
with other personae
      when I had different faces?

1977

TATTOO

When our son wanted an earring, his dad was cool—
even took him to get it; I was overruled.

Then Dad came home with his own ear pierced too;
I smiled and said, "It looks great on you."

Our son worked out and developed his abs;
Dad admired them and said they looked fab.

Then Dad started jogging and joined the gym;
I had to admit, his suits looked better on him.

When our son bought the styles of tomorrow,
Dad's body was fit and son's clothes he could borrow.

Then our son went and got a tattoo;
at first Dad was shocked, like at anything new.

But now Dad is stating, "I need to stay young.
I'll get a tattoo on my chest, here over my lung."

I nodded that it was fine and didn't say too much—
just that I'd forward his mail and to keep in touch.

Now that I've thought about it all for awhile,
I know when he sees my new tattoo, he will smile.

1989

Parenthood

We look at our children of any age

with pride in our breast,

knowing we did and gave

all we could, our best.

      Each time they bleed,

      our wounds ache too;

      each time they soar,

      we beam anew.

There's nothing like parenthood

to bring right up to the fore

the pride and pleasure we get

from our futures, our genes, our core.

      We'll always be there,

      in loving spirit, at least,

      to share each sorrow, each fall,

      each triumph, each feast.

RITA FIDLER DORN

PRISON

Locked in a prison of tradition,
shackled to old ways of doing and thinking.

Dwelling in the comfort and safety of the past,
in a land not relevant to the current world.

Unhappy, scared, tortured, but unable to break out,
unable or unwilling; maybe both.

Afraid to try anything new—styles, values, methods;
all loom ahead as terrifying risks.

Sad, suffering, discontent, miserable . . .
but not enough to change, or explore other options.

Easier to stand with fists clenched around
the jail bars, and wail.

Locked in tightly for a lifetime sentence,
with no key to the sunlight of change and growth.

How will I escape this prison when I get old?

SEX, THEN and NOW

Then it was urgent, intense, commanding.
Now it's sweet, appreciated, sometimes enough.

Then it was fierce, breathless, brash.
Now it's friendly, fragile, soft-spoken.

Then we were sure it would be that way forever.
Now we feel lucky when it's there at all.

Then we thought we'd be young for a century
and that sex belonged to us—our birthright, our personal property.

Now we and sex are good friends, close and fond,
but it no longer holds its former dominance over us.

Like any relationship, it changes with passing years:
buds, builds, peaks, holds steady, dims a bit, remains cherished.

2012

TOO YOUNG

Their eyes looked scared, their swaggers too pronounced;
still wet behind their ears, the world, their pouts denounced.

They covered two bar stools; their orders were too sure;
they seemed to fall apart, at the barmaid's slight allure.

Her glance was steady; her gentle smile ignored their plea;
softly, sweetly, she formed the words, "May I see your ID?"

1968

CITIES and OTHER PLACES

"You are a busy, bustling city in which an over-exposed identity many find anonymity and peace."

"Lonesome Cities (book by Rod McKuen): a fallacy because every city borders on at least a few other cities—just as no person can avoid touching or being touched by others, no man or city can possibly be an island."

ATLANTA, 1970: MY GOLDEN YEAR

My first year in Atlanta—I was now free
to develop, learn about, and reinvent me.
      To discover the person I might become,
        progress, for sure, in view of where I was from.
Independent, well able to roam
and embrace life, but on terms of my own.

      My studio apartment was sized for one;
      houseguests and parties anyhow, lots of fun.
Lava lamps and incense gave a mellow feel;
sangria punch with strips of cucumber peel.
      My yellow Ford Falcon, a Remington portable;
      I had abundant cash, so all was affordable.

Dogwood blossoms, and shoppers' feet,
Rich's famed store on Peachtree Street.
      The High Art Museum, a new Colony Square,
      Solarus Room restaurant revolved high in the air.
Hot young guys and comely babes;
Italian fare at arty Gene and Gabe's.

      Prestigous Emory U., of course,
      Academy Theatre's drama discourse.
At The Iron Horse: retsina and lamb meat;
mousakka, rich; baklava, gooey and sweet.
      Large and shrubby Piedmont Park
      always had action, in sunshine or dark.

Brought a TV and all my books—my treasures--
now ready to check out the Southern pleasures.
      Newly made friends and thrilling adventures,
      some spicy relationships, creative ventures.
Of all the good memories to which I'm beholden,
none match that time in Atlanta, a year so golden.

THE SAGA OF BROOKLYN

My dad was a blonde Brooklyn boy who fell
in love with a feisty girl from the Bronx—my mom;
she had jet black hair, and eyes full of fire;
right off, he was taken by her aplomb.

Ebbets Field and the Brooklyn Dodgers!!
Chubby mamas and old, wrinkled codgers
sat in the summertime out on the stoop,
while kids played stick ball and sang Loop-de-Loop.
In Brooklyn, they drew hopscotch on the sidewalk,
numbering with broken sticks of white chalk.

This borough boasts Pratt and the Prospect Park Zoo,
and delis that serve corned beef on rye for you.
The Brooklyn Museum won't be outdone.
You get best Chinese food: lo mein, chicken sub gum.

Candy stores and dress shops thrive under the El;
Erasmus and New Utrecht each rings its school bell.
But when my sweet tooth has a memory dream,
nothing beats a tall and friendly chocolate egg cream!

RITA FIDLER DORN

WINTER ON CAIN PARK HILL IN CLEVELAND

Parents' cars parked along the sidewalk are a tidy preamble to the
main attraction of sledding down the polished hill at the first snowfall.

Little faces are frozen in fear; mittened fists desperately clutch the parka
of the person in front.

Eyes widen hugely, as the children careen down the steep, smooth,
this-is-taking-forever hill.

On a sled, one or two; on a toboggan, three or four deep;
or a single in a huge round Frisbee thing, wishing she were not alone.

No steering wheel, no seat belt, no brakes, no horn.
Only directional tool is the front kid leaning way out and over
to the right or the left, veering the vehicle that way.
Each time, those behind him shriek hysterically.
A few of the littlest ones cry tears of uncontrollable afraid-ness.

When they reach the bottom, all tumbling out of their transport at once,
into the welcoming snow, arms and legs up in the air, and
colorful parkas and leggings intermingled—everyone screams,
"I wasn't scared." "Let's go back up and do it again!"

Little faces beam, forgotten tears not yet dry on their red cheeks.
The snow smells and feels good, even in chunks on soft, warm skin.

Wintertime in Cleveland, Ohio—Cain Park Hill is the place to be.

DRIVER'S PSALM

Caution's my shepherd; I shall not speed.
He makes me slow down at school crossings;
He leads me safely on six-lane highways.
He relaxes my passengers.
He guides me on icy roads and through blinding snowstorms.

Yea, though I cruise through the valley of careless motorists
        I will fear no accident, for Caution is with me.
My common sense and my emergency brake, they comfort me.

He has prepared me as a good example in the presence of
        reckless and ignorant drivers.
He has chosen to safeguard me with vigilant eyes;
        I am blessed.
Surely collision and traffic death shall shun me all my days on the road,
        if I drive by these precepts forever.

1961

—*written as an assignment for a journalism class*
    at Ohio State University

MEXICO BY MOTORCYCLE

One summer, I cycled across scenic Mexico,
with only small gas cans from stations like Texaco.

I spoke no *espanol w*hen I arrived,
but soon learned food words, so I could survive.
'Tho my friend and I planned one Acapulco week,
our trip became a 20-day vacation streak.

From Ballet Folklorico to outdoor markets selling rugs;
street vendors offered jewelry, *croquetas, cafe,* and drugs.
Mi amiga was *fluente y tienen novios* in every little city;
those guys were so much fun—energetic and witty.

Our last night there, a huge earthquake struck;
asleep, I thought it a dream and ignored it—my luck!
We flew home with memories of soup made of chicken and barley,
but my favorite part was that rented red and silver Harley !

BREEZY, SUNNY MIAMI BEACH

Breezy, sunny Miami Beach:
palm trees close enough to reach;
eat an orange or a peach.
> A place to put my dreams,
> coffee with flavored creams,
> children's playful screams.
> That's so Miami.

Multi-colored skirts,
multi-cultural teenaged flirts,
disappointment that really hurts.
> A street off Lincoln *Road not taken,*
> Bond's martini, stirred not shaken,
> aroma from the oven, cookies bakin'.
> That's so Miami.

A motorboat scooting across the bay,
motorcycles whooshing at end of day,
motorized wheelchairs on their way.
> Tattoo parlors open all night,
> muscled hoodlums in a fight,
> dying people, approaching the light.
> That's so Miami.

*One of my That's So Miami submissions
that was posted on the O Miami website
during National Poetry Month, April 2013.*

FEAST ON, MIAMI

That's so Miami, all that's here:
Parties and skateboards; friends drinking beer.

They come from London for fun in the sun,
but hope to avoid a burn on the "bum."

Oliver's, Shorty's, and Seasons 52
serve up a taste of Miami for you.

Brazilian barbeque and Taco Bell
make *Cariocas* and *Mexicanos* welcome, as well.

Blue Martini swings and sparkles at night;
Outback's Blooming Onions taste just right.

If you crave the melting pot flavor
and memories you hope to savor,

it's lush and wondrous, like a double whammy!
Whatever you eat here is so Miami!!

One of my That's So Miami submissions
that was posted on the O Miami website
during National Poetry Month, April 2013

STORE WINDOWS BOARDED UP

Store windows boarded up,
litter on the sidewalks, empty beer cans,
a broken bike parked morosely against a tree.
A dream not deferred, but totally forgotten.
Hope given up for dead.

>Coral Gables counterpart
>boasts manicured lawns and
>sports cars in the driveways.
>Kids walk to school in new shoes and clean clothes.
>High expectations, demanding to be met.

Two inhabitants of the same city,
like roommates who come to college
from different corners of the world,
anticipating harmony and friendship.
Whose world will rub off on the other?
That's so Miami.

2013

*One of my That's So Miami submissions
that was posted on the O Miami website
during National Poetry Month, April 2013.*

STONECRABS AT JOE'S

That's so Miami, eating stone crabs at Joe's;
snowbirds arrive and traffic slows.
      Espadrilles and a cotton sundress;
      rain showers lasting five minutes or less.

Sidewalk art shows, Coconut Grove,
loomers hawking rugs they wove.
      Miami Dade, UM, FIU;
      the Dolphins to their colors stay true.

Naming new hurricane storms?
Shuttered windows are the norm.
      Excellent plays at GableStage;
      dinner at Shula's—still the rage!

Summer humidity gives no relief?
Head to the Keys and a coral reef.
      South Beach parades diverse humanity;
      surf or water ski; preserve your sanity.

Small aircraft at Tamiami,
that, too, is so Miami!

One of my That's So Miami submissions
that was posted on the O Miami website
during National Poetry Month, April 2013.

MONDAY MORNING BUS RIDE

Two too-high steps, welcoming riders on board
Black rubber-matted floors
     which have coupled with millions of shoes
Ravished seats
     of soft, old, sweaty leather
Crowded aisles
     filled with swaying figures
     of traveling humanity
The screech of rubber tires
     assaulting the pavement outside,
     still hot and weary from summer
Strangers pushing against each other,
     stepping on toes,
     indifferent to their invasion of the other one's space
The robot of a driver,
     who barely turns his head to the right
     in reply to a friendly rider's "Good morning"
     or to the left to nod back at a fellow driver's hand
     raised in lackadaisical greeting
The odor of whiskey
     from a not-quite outgrown hangover
The sleeveless, hairy underarms
     standing above you,
     reeking putrid perspiration
The deli smell of
     a salami and mustard sandwich
     hiding in a creased paper bag
The dark tie and white shirt of the man
     on his way to a new job

     RITA FIDLER DORN

The weary, desperate smile
    of the thin, elderly lady,
    in a well-worn, navy blue suit
The tired teenager,
    carrying a few unwelcome books,
    sporting a tattoo and a scowl.
The sounds, the smells, the sights . . . .
    always engrossing.
The ritual of the bus ride,
    always the same, always different.

1961

CONFLICT

"We must not allow other people's limited perceptions to define us."
—Virginia Satir

"You don't get points for suffering."
—Corbin Dorn

"Not everyone is entitled to have a front seat in your life.
Some people need to sit in the balcony and
you need to make sure they stay there."
—Unknown

"If you were a car, I'd make lemonade out of you."
—R.F. Dorn

DANCING TO MUSIC
I DON'T WANT TO HEAR

Dancing to music I don't want to hear,
humming the words I don't like,
swaying to the beat of an enemy drum;
it will never be all right.

The tempo surrounds my being;
alien melody invades my brain;
everyone else is smiling to the song
—only I am in this pain.

I want to hear some different notes,
tunes which mirror my true desires,
but long before the song is over,
my vision of hope has expired.

FORGIVE

First we anger,
and then we blame;
next we yell, and
quit the game.
     Let go of the anger;
     let go of its name.
     Release to the wind
     all of the blame.
When we've been wronged,
we harbor the hurt;
we feel so low,
like a pile of dirt.
     We wallow and weep
     and nurture the pain,
     although we know
     there's nothing to gain.
Forgive, they tell us,
but it's not so easy.
Can we do it?
Makes us feel queasy.
     Forgiveness is
     the one way to heal,
     to get on with our lives,
     and once more be real.
So let go of the anger,
let go of its name.
Release to the wind
every bit of the blame.

2002

          RITA FIDLER DORN

FIGHTING THE FIGHTS

Fighting the fight
to stay asleep all night,
waking at 2, at 3, and at 4,
unable to lie abed any more.

Fighting the fight with scale and weight,
haunted by yesterday's food that I ate,
with jeans that shrank in the blink of an eye,
and all for the sake of a thin slice of pie.

Fighting the fight with people I love,
I act like a lion more than a dove;
conflict with those whom once I adored,
who now enrage me or make me bored.

Rememb'ring when we
were on the same page . . .
fighting the fight with
time and with age.

Battling a world that perversely has changed,
I no longer feel at *"home on the range,"*
wandering in a world that refuses to please,
wondering why somebody *"moved my cheese!"*

What time is it now? Where is the light?
What must I do to get this right?
Need my Owner's Manual to see
whether I am still in warranty.

Just Wanted To Share

They just wanted to share about their weekend of fun:
the party they went to, and their day in the sun.
Just wanted to share about a concert they thought was swell,
of a new restaurant they tried, and a joke he could tell.
>   They did not bore you with details of their health,
>   or the robber who came and stole some of their wealth.
>   They didn't ask you to put up their hurricane shutters
>   or help them clean the garage of stuff which clutters.

She just wanted to share a home-cooked dinner
or about a game she played in which she was the winner.
He just wanted to show you an award that he earned,
thus, reaching a goal for which he'd long yearned.
>   Didn't tell you of a few debts that they owe,
>   or their strain to recall stuff—they're aging, you know.
>   Didn't list for you the meds they are taking,
>   the doctors they see, or their aches upon waking.

Just wanted to catch a movie with you or watch the game,
share a beer and a romp with their puppy, whom they're trying to train.
They wished that you'd share some real news of your life,
but your silence and distance cut like a knife.
>   Didn't request help with decisions or technology,
>   but when speaking to you, they must use psychology.
>   Didn't recount their challenges with sight and hearing,
>   or some future issues which they might be fearing.

Just wanted to see you a little bit more,
and often hoped you'd come to their door.
They just wanted to spend some hours with you,
so you'd feel loved when they were through.

> Didn't admit that for you they are lonely
> or remind you that you are their "only."
> But you were busy or in other places,
> and had small interest in seeing their faces.

WHAT LIVES INSIDE OF YOU?

You lie, you cheat, you curse, you steal.
You inflict wounds that will never heal.

Beneath our surface conflicts
you harbor no respect or love;
your occasional, tender efforts
are just a façade, like a glove.

With no binding interest
in who we are or what we face,
or in the chemistry we share,
you doggedly march to your own pace.

No sympathy for man or beast
or the pain in another's heart.
The only demands that you can hear
are ones that you impart.

The efforts of those who love you
are discarded like pieces of trash;
their commitment to you will soon
disappear in the wind, like ash.

Right and wrong, truth and lies—
you see them in identical hue.
How did you get to be that way?
What lives inside of you?

1990

HARSH WORDS

We exchanged harsh words
that cut like swords;
    our egos were bruised and bloody.
Insults, hurled like darts,
pierced our hearts;
    our emotions were now all muddy.

The very next day,
I went back to say,
    "I'm sorry," but you weren't there.
I looked around;
there was no sound;
    you had vanished into thin air.

I sought a new chance,
or a quick, friendly glance,
    an opportunity to repair
the damage that was done,
by the setting of the sun
    but the battlefield now was bare.

2002

KALEIDOSCOPE

I feel the pressure in my head,
as if I were inside a kaleidoscope,
amid all those colors raining down on me.

The colors and sounds interface
to create visual and audible chaos.
The chaos envelopes me and I absorb its fury.

I try to get out, but I can't;
I want to organize the shapes, but I don't;
I hate to be at the mercy of their threats, but I am.
I want them to fade away, but they won't.

Will I live in the kaleidoscope forever?

2006

THEY HAD A DREAM

They had a dream that their four little boys
would grow up to be their pride and joys,

who'd mature into fine young men—
admirable and honest, so sure of it then;

who'd respect each other and stay ever close,
sharing relationships of which they could boast.

A loving family who grows and thrives
is one who cherishes each others' lives.

They nurtured that dream, sure it would come true;
it was the reality held as their due.

But along the path, they lost their way;
it became hard to see from day to day.

And when the fog cleared, a lot had changed:
the four young sons had become estranged,

apart from each other and from parents as well,
without any sound, or the toll of a bell.

It happened in daylight without cover of dark;
with no words spoken, the boys put out the spark,

the spark of love and future hopes.
Now everyone's tangled in emotional ropes.

WALKING AWAY

when we tried and tried, and tried our best, and then tried some more,
when we made no progress at all, could not get a foot in the door,
when we cried and laughed, threatened and bribed, pleaded and swore,
our egos and confidence were splattered all over the floor.
we knew we had to walk away.

it still wouldn't work, but the memories lurked;
no efforts were shirked, and failure still perked.
we gave it all we had, and even what we didn't;
we displaced it and spaced it, ignored it, abhorred it.
we hated to walk away.

when we tried and tried, and tried our best, and then tried some more,
when our egos were low enough to be mopping the floor;
when we made no progress at all, and it still didn't work,
we hated the fact that bad mem'ries lurked.
our days were dark and our nights were worse;
we'd have given anything to shift into reverse.
we had to walk away.

when we tried and tried, and tried our best, and then we tried some more,
when we came to the point in the road where there was no place to go,
when we cried and laughed, threatened and bribed, pleaded and swore,
there was no more to say and no more to think, and it was all just gore.
we still hated to walk away.

when we had no more strength, no truth, no hope,
we ached to escape but still couldn't cope;
we were worn from fatigue and depressed from pain,
but knew more efforts, too, would be in vain.
we had no spark left, just profound distress,
devastated that we could get no success.
we had to walk away . . . . but we will always look back.

RITA FIDLER DORN

PEACE and WAR

Food among the flowers, flowers in the field.
A separate peace amid the wars.
Slices of sadness.
Remembering war, and its results,
terrorism and its consequences,
shredded lives and broken futures surviving like ancient ruins.
Still striding toward peace, unity, contentment,
but always under the watchful auspices of war,
trying to ignore the threat of its dastardly damage.
Determined to achieve congeniality among nations,
despite the underpinnings of discontent, distrust, and greed.
Sometimes questioning whether it's worth it, fighting for peace,
knowing peace is right, but haggling over the price it exacts.

2011

LOVE, ETC.

"Love means your soul has found its home."
—R.F. Dorn

"Hope is the thing with feathers, that perches in the soul."
—Emily Dickinson

*"You are like a cloud on which the restless gull in me can light,
calm but just lilting enough to stay interesting."*
—Unknown

LOVE SHORTIES

If I'd have never met you and
our paths had never crossed,
I'd have loved you, anyhow.

If they really love you,
when you get old,
they still think you are pretty.

Love is private and public,
sour and sweet, internal and external, silent and loud,
intense and serene, concrete and fluid,
fleeting and eternal.

I feel so secure with your hand in mine,
like an ivy leaf, on a climbing vine.

Love is the flicker of a candle flame,
the only part that counts.

A PEACH and A PLUM

How do I love you? Let me count the days:

MONDAY-   My body lies next to yours,
your heart beats close to mine,
two souls in perfect harmony
of rhythm, stroke, and time.

TUESDAY-   A peach and a plum,
forefinger and thumb,
Daphnis and Chloe,
pizza crust crisp; cheese doughy.

WEDNESDAY-   Like Tristram and Isolde,
penicillin and mold,
oaty cereal with milk,
bed clothes woven out of silk.

THURSDAY-   A pair, a unit, a team,
a sentence complete,
a symphony perfect,
with no missing beat.

FRIDAY-   Talking fast and raptly listening,
working out and wetly glistening,
long and yearning tender glances,
smooth, romantic, graceful dances.

SATURDAY-   Shoot a few baskets together
in the sunny autumn weather;
champagne afternoon delight,
cozy picnic at midnight.

SUNDAY-   Facing crises, delighting in joys,
sweet quietude, cacophonous noise;
sharing quick breakfasts, leisurely dinners;
in this combo, we both are the winners.

1970, 2013

BEING MARRIED TO YOU

We can't imagine where the years have flown.
Yes, we're older now and our children are grown.

You say that I look about the same;
I smile and answer, "What's your game?"

I know that can't possibly be true,
but that's how I feel when I look at you.

> You made me laugh 'til my sides hurt; I felt good about life;
> we shared so many passions, so I said I'd be your wife.
>
> You made me feel content with the place I was in;
> you made me feel clever; you even made me feel thin.
>
> When I review our life and the years together,
> I'm pleased we're still wed, despite some stormy weather.

You vowed, "With you, I want to grow old;
we'll never let the fire go out or see our love get cold."

We played with our kids; we read the same books;
and we still banter with words and flirtatious looks.

I am grateful for our life and this moment in time,
even the challenges, and the many sweet glasses of wine!

2010

Good Morning, I Love You

Good morning, I love you.
I love how you look
when you open your eyes each day,
how you look when you get out of the shower
with drops of water all over your hunky body.
Good night, I love you.
I love how you smell when you come to bed,
your sexy fragrance filling our bedroom.
Sweet dreams, I love you.
I love how you sound, breathing evenly in the bed, next to me.
Sleep tight, I love you.
I love how you feel when my toes touch yours.
How your arm skims the top of my head and comes around my shoulder,
signaling, "Let's cuddle."
I love waking up in the middle of the night to feel your warmth beside me.
I love having another day of my life to spend with you.
Good morning, I love you.

2011

I Always Knew You

I knew you before crossing paths in this life;
I always knew I'd become your wife.

Visions of you filled my girlhood dreams;
love, hope, and laughter were the themes.

I saw your face in the thoughts of my youth;
I knew you were my future, my truth.

I waited impatiently for the passage of years
to actually hear your voice in my ears.

I always knew
I'd find my way to you.

2001, 2004

LOVE MEANS

Love means caring, sharing,
gently preparing

It's ever turning, always yearning,
oft discerning

Sometimes fussing, even cussing,
and lots of discussing

Sleeping and weeping with,
frowning and clowning with . . . .

Together and alone,
love means
your soul has found its home.

OF ALL THE MEN . . . .

Of all the men I've ever known,
none, my soul, could dare to own.
> Of all the ones who crossed my path,
> not one gave my heart a rose petal bath.
Of all the men who made my mood swell,
none connected with my brain so well.
> Of the men who challenged me,
> not one my values could set free.
Of those who followed me in rain,
none erased old scars and pain.
> Of the many with whom I spoke,
> none, my visions, could revoke.
Of all the ones who sang with me,
none blended with my melody.
> Of all the men I've ever known,
> none, my soul, did dare to own.
> Except for you.

2011

LIFE ON HOLD

I tell myself that I must do right,
that tomorrow and hope loom ahead and bright;
I tell myself to think rationally too,
but all I can think about is you.

I tell myself that things will improve,
but meanwhile I must get in the groove.
I must overcome the angst and the pain,
and attempt to start to live again.

I tell myself all the things I should,
to move on with my life—I wish I could.
Surely there must be some way
to regain sanity and peace today.

Everyone tells me that again the sun will shine,
and serenity will once more be mine.
Perhaps, but now I sing a somber song;
I honestly don't think I can wait that long.

The road ahead is dark and full of fright;
I see no sign that I will surpass this blight.
Despair fills me from toes to my face;
I don't want to spend "always" in this lonely space.

1968

AT MY VERY BEST

You see me at my very best,
with perfume on and full of zest,
away from kids and household dust,
unmade beds, and fender rust.

Away from Sunday's eating binge,
baby's squalls, and a squeaky hinge,
away from Monday morning blues—
that's my life; I pay my dues.

From Tuesday's broken washing machine—
the repairman, an old guy, grizzled and mean;
from Wednesday's tears and money stress,
from errands, dishes, shirts to press.

You see me at my very best,
with perfume on and full of zest,
away from kids and household dust,
sexy, smiling, full of lust.

Away from Thursday night's depression
and Friday's kid with math regression,
from Saturday morning's dentist bill,
and hubby's hangover, lingering still.

RITA FIDLER DORN

You see me at my very best,
fresh and sparkling, riding the crest;
you know just a mere façade of me,
a person I never thought I'd be.

If you saw me at my worst,
inside my bubble, ready to burst,
a very different face you'd view—
but that's the "me" that would be true.

You see me at my very best,
with perfume on and full of zest,
away from kids and household dust,
unmade beds and fender rust.

REALISTIC LOVE SONG

Love only me, with each new dawning day;
bring me morning coffee in your sweet and gentle way.
Kiss me on the shoulder as you tell me once again,
how you'll love me for forever, 'til the lark deserts the glen.

Hold my hand and squeeze it as we're walking in the dark;
dream the dreams I dream for you and kiss me in the park.
Laugh with me and love me; watch all the things we share
grow stronger while the days go by . . . our love will keep them fair.

Pray that we grow together, but, if somehow, we do not,
far better that we smile and part, than to endure the hurt.
So, many memories from now, in some nostalgic mood,
we can reflect upon this love and say that it was good.

Now let us not just wonder what the future holds in store;
let's give it all we've got today and just a little more.
But when the lark has flown the glen and our hearts hold no regrets,
we'll just kiss good-bye and say, "Those years were all the best!"

Love only me, with each new dawning day;
bring me morning coffee in your sweet and gentle way.
Kiss me on the shoulder as you tell me once again,
how you'll love me for forever, 'til the lark deserts the glen.

1970, 1985

THIS MAN

He is my type, he smokes no pipe,
he wears his clothes too loosely.
He lives by the clock, he leans toward Bach,
he speaks his mind profusely.

His eyes show grief, his kiss is brief,
his compliments come slowly.
He walks in sun, is sometimes fun;
he is good but far from holy.

He is my friend, my foe, my end,
my turmoil, and my lever.
Though our worlds collide, I'm sure that I
will be his love forever.

1968

RITA FIDLER DORN

CRINKLNG EYES ABOVE A SMILE

Crinkling eyes above a smile
becoming laughter in awhile.
Sensuous voice, rich and mellow,
engaging from the first hello.
Always with the sharpest wit;
for me, every date a hit.

Glass of wine in a quiet spot,
something there that could get hot.
Jazz concerts, sidewalk art shows;
warming cheeks and sunset glows.
Long drives, loose hand holding,
personalities unfolding.

Corduroy slacks with jacket's tweed;
worthy dialogue on which to feed.
Candle in the autumn dusk,
fragrance smelling strong of musk.
Buying books, seeing plays;
cool nights, brightest days.

Pipe tobacco—Cherry Blend;
conflicting messages to send.
Subtle signals there to heed;
should my heart prepare to bleed?
We didn't stand time's rigid test,
but my memories hold no requests.

1969

YOU ARE THE ONE

The earth is the boundary of where I can walk,
but you are the one with whom I best talk:
You give me answers I'd never conceive,
new dreams and goals in which to believe.

Offering responses which complement me,
you are the leaves on my emotional tree.
You touch my heart, my psyche, my core;
you are my mirror, my essence, but more.

I feel grateful for being alive;
with you as my partner, we will thrive.
One life now, where once there were two—
I can't imagine living mine without you.

1971

TWO PLANETS ONCE

We that two planets once had been
are now a double star,
and in the heavens may be seen
where we connected are.

Whirled with subtle power along,
into new space we enter,
and, evermore, with spheral song
revolve about one center.

1961

THE SPARK OF LOVE

What is love made of? What ignites the spark?
A look, a touch, an emotion?
A shared moment, the perfect word, or
a concurred opinion?
A caress, an embrace, a kiss brief or lingering.
A piece of music shared and savored.
A solution to a challenge. A golden triumph.
One smile and a responding one.
An aroma, fresh or long treasured.
What kindles the spark, keeps it glowing,
or puts it at risk to go dark? Nobody knows.
Hard to define, but bask in the sparkle of it anyhow,
as long as it brightens your life.

2013

Remembering

"Consciousness survives death."
—Holly W. Schwartztol, Ph. D.

"Death is my least favorite part of life."
—R.F. Dorn

A 60's Chick

They called girls "Chick,"
took us to the Flick,
a coffee house, Miami South.

The mood was mellow,
no one would bellow;
cool tones came from our mouth.

Guitar music claimed our souls,
we ate thin soup from metal bowls;
the bill was small; the need was thrift.

The smoke was thick,
but not enough to get sick . . .
if you get my drift.

Evenings were dark,
clothing was stark;
the stance was anti-estab.

We felt tranquil and high
as we drummed on our thigh
and tried to connect and collab.

CASHEWS

I eat cashew nuts in memory of my mother
who loved cashews.
When I was a little girl,
we would go into Morrow's Nut Shop, and
she would buy a quarter pound of warm cashews
in a small, white paper bag.
As we walked along the street,
of busy downtown Cleveland,
she held the bag and gave me some
every time she took a few for herself.
I wanted to hold the bag sometimes
but I never asked, and she never offered it to me.
Only the nuts, cashew nuts.
I eat them now in memory of her.

2007

WHEN IT RAINS

when it rains, i think of you and me
running through the torrents of my childhood,
safe and dry beneath the security of that big umbrella.

when it snows, i think of you
shoveling drifts from our driveway,
so Dad could pull his car in when he came home.

when it's sunny out, i think of you packing a lunch
for us to enjoy on the grass of a park called Strawberry Lane,
in the summers of my youth.

when it's dark and late at night, i relive
the midnight games of Scrabble at our kitchen table.

when it's early in the morning, i recall you
waking me up to get dressed, to start on a family vacation.

when it' s a holiday, i think of you
on all the special occasions we shared, and took for granted.

when it's everyday, i miss you.
when it hurts, i cry.

you left a lasting imprint on my heart.

2001

CANDLE IN MY DARK

You were the candle in my dark.
You were the picnic in my park.
You were the music of my soul.

You helped me learn to make my way.
You taught me to structure every day.
You were the one who made me whole.

Your humor and your raunchy jokes
laughter from our hearts evoked.
You played piano: classics, jazz, rock 'n roll.

We cooked, we laughed, we went on cruises;
you gave me praise and kissed my bruises.
You told me I must always have a goal.

You loved my poems but hated my sewing;
your all-time motto was, "Gotta keep going!"
You ate pickled herring on an onion roll.

Confidante, mentor, opinion giver:
Brisk and sweet as a cool, spring river.
In my dreams, you will never get old.

You were the candle in my dark.
You were the picnic in my park.
My memories of you will never grow cold.

You promised me you'd never die . . . .
You lied.

2001 in memory of my mother,
Beatrice Greenberg Fidler 1911-2000.

WHAT COLOR IS SADNESS?

What color is sadness?
>How does it appear?
>Does it make you shed a tear?

What's the timbre of its voice?
As if we even had a choice.
>Does the sound
>retreat or abound?

What is the texture of sadness?
>Melancholy smooth, recalling lost youth?
>Or scratchy and rough? . . . Enough is enough!

What is the mood of sadness?
>How does it feel? How do we know?
>How long will it stay? How soon will it go?

What is the flavor of sadness?
>Do you chew or swallow it? How does it taste?
>Can we expel it in disgust and in haste?

What is the scent of sadness?
>How does it smell?
>Does it entice us, or offend and repel?

The color, the feel, the taste, sound, and smell
are foes whose armies we can't always quell.
>What color is sadness, for you?

2001

TWILIGHT

In the twilight of your life,
we walked together

through the
sometimes murky days and nights.

You leaned on me for support,
like I leaned on you when I was little.

Our way was illuminated by
the sweet visions
of healthier, younger times.

And now, you too,
are among the memories of my life,

lighting it
with the strength of your spirit
and the unique, never-ending love

that a parent harbors for a child, of any age.

HE

He is a mortal man,
  not a god or supreme being.
He is only human,
  but he means everything to me.

He is tall and fair,
  his blue eyes atwinkle with humor.
He has heart
  and deepest understanding.
He is stern in judgment,
  though always just.

I feel his presence
  when he is near.
Though his heart is gold,
  he squanders neither time nor money.

To me, he is a king . . . .
  for he is my father.

1958

RITA FIDLER DORN

SEASONS, TIME, and WEATHER

"Some people walk in the rain and enjoy the raindrops;
others just get wet."
— **Roger Miller**

"If I were the wind I'd carry the world to a far-off place."
— **R.F. Dorn**

"Earth is where I keep my stuff."
— **Unknown**

"Use the good china every day."
— **Corbin Dorn**

MORNING

Some days I wake up rested, limber,
        ready to jump into the day ahead;
others I awake achy, cranky, sour.

Some days I am eager to greet the tasks
        of the next 24 hours;
on others, I crave to return to the cave,
        of my bed and stick my head
        under the pillow for refuge.

Some days I bound out of bed,
        open, with the energy of expectation;
on others, I rise slowly, morosely, reluctantly,
        not in any rush.

On some, I awake grateful to have woken up,
        and not died in the dark, appreciating the
        impermanence of the ritual nocturnal nap;
on others, I put my feet on the floor slowly,
        my warm soles gingerly touching
        its smooth coldness.

Either way, after awhile, I regress to the mean.
If initially exuberant,
        I settle into the day with *nonchalance*;
if at first pouty, I improve,
        reaching an oasis of pleasant acceptance.

I greet morning with many faces.

ETERNAL LOVE

The tide splashes generously
upon the beach,
like jelly on children's clothing.
Each drop of water
holds captive a pearl of light.
The arms of the sea
abandon and revisit the shore
in an unrelenting love affair.

1988

SUNRISE

The sunrise at dawn
is a breathtaking sight,
  as the arrival of morn
  greets the departure of night.

The whole earth appears
so completely at peace;
  if only this haven
  never would cease.

But, alas, for already,
as clear as the dew,
  one more perfect day
  has started anew.

1958

THE SUN LEAVES
ITS WARMTH ON ME

The sun leaves its warmth on me, embossing
its gentle imprint on my face—I flush;
on my arms—they responsively reach upward;
on my back—it stretches luxuriously;
on my shins and ankles who are cavalier about the sun;
and on my toes—which wiggle in glee.

The sun's rays, which traveled so far to visit,
deserve the attention I would show any guest.

First, I welcome its nourishing properties
of feeding the grass, flowers, and trees.

Then, I praise it for the light it offers each earthly day.

But next, I must protect myself from its predatory interest in my skin—
so vulnerable to the sun's power that they cannot be left alone
without the chaperones of Sunscreen and Sunblock.

Finally, I cherish the golden joy of the sunshine,
and let its positive rays brighten my attitude.
The sun, indeed, leaves its warmth on me.

Long After the Rain

What can I wear? What's up with my hair?
Put on my shoes . . . Now, ready to cruise.

Looking for love in whatever places,
losing myself in unlikely spaces.

Hoping for others to make me feel whole,
to help me establish a meaningful goal.

But still *"tossed and driven,"* I swirl down the drain,
like water disposed of, long after the rain.

2012

THE RAIN and ME

I love the rain,
watching it rush down from the clouds
to quench the earth's thirst,
feed the grass and the flowers,
vitalize the trees.

I see the families of drops,
grouped together in trim columns,
hurrying to their destinations,
their urgency unexplained.

Even from my window, I feel its power.
When I walk beneath it, I am within it,
part of the wet; refreshed and cleansed,
believing, for those moments,
that I am safe under its thin, nurturing blanket.

2012

4 HAIKU

early MORN waking
to a day of new choices,
made only for me.

MINUTES, hours, weeks
amble, then gallop, on streets
of our lives; we watch.

SUMMER voices buzz,
twitter, hiss, splash; someone yells,
"Come in for lunch, now!"

my face smiles broadly;
success spreads through my body;
my soul is content.

WEATHER STATION 5.7.5

Snowflakes are God's way
to play with water and ice,
and share them with us.

      Gold beams, rays, cancer
      of the skin. Sun worshipping
      is not worth the price.

Raindrops falling on
my collar and my hairdo
and also on you.

      Fog blurs the driver's
      view of the street; hope he is
      not in back of me.

Slush is merely snow
and ice mixed with rain, ready
for the crunch of boots.

      Wind: the propellant
      of leaves on the sidewalk which
      become a flurry.

Smog was industry's
fog-smoke combo in London;
now has chemicals.

QUARTET OF RIVERS

RIVER #1: Quiet and tranquil, full of winding bends;
caressing bare shorelines before it ends.
Embankments with trees, graceful and tall,
create a leafy pathway in a tree-bark hall.

RIVER #2: Large and bouldered, islet-studded;
turbulent waters, abundantly mudded.
Shrubs along the coastline; rocky, diverging streams;
small cliffs like ancient ruins: a place for measured dreams.

RIVER #3: A river low and narrow; its other side a distant shore;
shallow and deep surround the peaks; mysterious, filled with lore.
Impassioned and untamed, a refuge, yet bare as stone.
A lone orchid blossom on the bank—independent, far from home.
With colossal potential, it brims with brutal power,
a place where victories are remembered, by the hour.

RIVER #4: Teeming with current, with people, with life;
a bridge, a few boats, laughter, no visible strife.
Swimmers and waders, picnics and litter;
flat rocks, whitecaps, and sea drops that glitter.
Waters that open up the heart; rejuvenation and rebirth;
this river is a lively contrast to the stillness of the earth.

1969, 2011

To Son Away At College

To my son, so dear,
you seem so near
when, late at night,
I turn on the light
in your room
to chase the gloom
of your not being here.

Yet, when you are home
from where you roam
we hassle and fight
over who is right
and who is wrong
and it's so hard to get along,
but don't be alone.

Come back to us soon
and fill up your room
with music and paint
and girls—you're no saint—
and smelly shoes and wrinkled clothes
and gallons of hair gel "wherever he goes."
spread your wings; shed your cocoon.

I turn off the light
and look up in the night
to see the stars on your ceiling glow,
and wonder what they know
about you and your plans as you lay in this bed
and the thoughts that were broadcast inside of your head.
I wish you a future North Star bright.

1993

SAY IT NOW

if you have words for one you care about
say it now and say it clearly; do not shout,
but say it well, so there is no doubt.

say it so that person hears it
and so you know you have said it;
say it again and again;
feel free to rethread it.

say it so the person must signal
that he or she heard it from you—
no matter what the response
or what that listener decides to do.

have a question for that person? ask.
it's your quest, your mission, your task.
make sure to get a reply from her or from him—
don't let the answer get lost in the din.

for hems and haws and "i'm not sure"
—asking the question can be a cure.

because when the person is dead
there's no more chance to ask, in the stead
of a life that is through—
no more interaction for you two.

RITA FIDLER DORN

can't hear you; can't answer; you'll never know,
and that's such a painful blow.

you'll never get to plant that seed,
despite your passion or your need;
so ask it now and right out loud;
don't wait; don't be timid or too proud.

ask it so you know that they hear
and must acknowledge that you were near,
and cared enough to say it or ask;
that's your mission; that's your task.

because when it's finished, it's over and done,
and becomes a battle that can never be won;
there'll be no place to run or to hide,
not even the forests, no matter how big your stride.
so, say it now!

2009

TRIBUTE TO AUTUMN

I can yet recall the beauties of this season
in Ohio, where I grew up . . . .
the first, tentative slivers of chill,
the deepening hues of leaves,
shorter days,
cashmere-corduroy-and-tweed,
and red plaid flannel blankets.
Of course, we sipped hearty soup,
and basked in the warming comfort
of marshmallowed hot chocolate,
heralded by its seductive aroma.

From our brick, well-lit family home,
we peered out of the windows at night
to watch the swaying tree branches
keep time to the piano music inside.

Horseback riding in the woods;
bonfires, hay rides, square dances;
and singing on the school bus
as we rode home from nighttime football games—
these are now pages in the scrapbook of my memory.

I can still know autumn, as I recall
my walks across the midwestern college campus, at dusk,
and feel the waning day
match stride with the fleeting season.

In any clime,
autumn bears an elegant tranquility
which pales before the holidays approach;
it is brisker than the expectancy of spring
and more purposeful than the indolent sweat of summer.

To autumn, an uplifting time of new semesters
and last chance resolves,
here's to you.

1996

RITA FIDLER DORN

HOLIDAY SKIES

Winter holidays brighten the sky,
bridging the space between the mind and the eye,
　　expanding perspective, stretching our view
　　between what we think and what we can do.
A touch of festivity, a bit of divinity,
but mostly the concept of pure infinity.

*2013 First Place at South Florida
Writers Association Poetry Write-in*

SELVES

"Allow yourself to go to that sacred place within yourself where you keep the treasure that is called by your name."
— **Virginia Satir**

"Always ask yourself, 'Is there another way I can look at this?' "
— **Anita Waller**

"You always regret the stuff you didn't do."
— **Corbin Dorn**

ALL I HAVE IS ME

When the problems and the pressures
start piling up on me . . . .
when the laments and the laundry
get so high that I can't see . . . .
when the hungries and the hassles
invade my liberty . . . .
It's then I must remember
that all I have is me.

A husband may pack up or die;
the kids will grow up soon;
but for my own survival
I always must make room.
My body and my mind
must be pampered faithfully,
because when all is said and done . . .
all I have is me.

1976

IMAGINE

Imagine that you are the person
whom you always yearned to be.
Finally.
Go to that place inside your heart
where you keep the stuff
that only you can know.
Respond to thoughts which speak to you.
Connect. Relate. Make it beautiful.
Peace will emerge and smooth the edges of your reverie.
Live long and love lustily.
Keep that mood when you return to earth,
for it will sustain you and be your strength.
Imagine.

2012

BE THE ARTIST OF YOUR LIFE

Be the artist of your life.
Sketch in the joy and make the sunshine big.
Color in happiness; use a lot of space.
Highlight the ecstasy with wide, bold strokes.

Paint in the rain, but not too much.
Smudge the colors of grief, to soften them.
Use some strong tones, for they are coping skills.
Spray on a coat of gloss to add stability.

Then frame it, and
hang it up to look at and enjoy.
You are the artist of your life.

2001

BLUES SONG

I've got it in my head,
though it's not on very straight,
that I've got to make some bread
before it grows too late.

My mind's a little foggy,
but I know what I must do;
my shoes are somewhat soggy;
can I get through to you?

Another gig gone down the drain,
another chance has splintered;
another dude has caused me pain,
another year has wintered.

Supposing that I gave up 'ludes
and saved my coins from day to day,
I've no education and all my moods
would surely get in the way.

I grew up stealing, went to dealing,
never was one much for school . . .
always loved to sing and swing,
I always could be cool.

But my cupboard's now bare,
and good friends are rare;
if I cleaned up and got dressed,
no one's here to impress.

What's the point? There's only gold;
I'm starting to feel I could grow old.
And if I'm good for one or two days,
I'd still live in my own lonely haze.

1970, 1981

A FEEL-GOOD DAY

a feel-good day, just for me—I deserve it.
e-mail in the morning, a few phone calls to friends.
made a luncheon date for Wednesday.
     I will revel in this Spring Break week and enjoy it to the max;
I'll bask in all that pleases me and put those issues and people who don't
     in a folder labeled, "Deal With Later."
I'll post happy scenes on my mental computer screen and be energized;
     today, I will devote myself to activities of choice.
ordered some sexy toys on line.
pizza for breakfast, diet Coke for a snack, and a green salad lunch;
     my new mantra: "low calorie; fat free; wise choice foods for me."
     (*I'm trying*.)
this week, I'll love my body and celebrate my soul,
sing while I'm doing chores,
expect the best, but weather the worst,
     make smart decisions (*pay attention*) and
     suck in all the mellow I can muster.
finally went to the gym; fragrant oils in the shower afterward; nice.

a feel-good day.
wear something pretty,
read something deep,
play the piano,
think about law school, again.
I chant my Hebrew lesson in preparation for my adult *bat mitzvah*.
     I feel like an old *Chasid*, both of us loving the prayers and
     rich heritage we share.
I love my house and organizing it (*control*)
I plan dinner (*delight in feeding my family*)
I smooth the corner of my bedspread and smile.
looking at photographs of my children, I smile again, inside and out.
I watch a blackbird splash in our bird bath, walk outside to smell a
     gardenia, note jewels of sunlight on the ripples in our pond.
inside, I flip through a book of Salvador Dali's art and let his paintings stir me.
     I write a poem about one. then, I sing *Tapestry* along with Carole King and
     hum Andrew Lloyd Weber's *Music of the Night*. (*their sounds are awesome*.)
called my honey at his office to say hi and to hear his voice.
this is **a feel-good day**. just for me. I'll try to make it feel good all day.

1998

STOP THE WORLD

Stop the world.
I don't want to get off.
I just want to rest awhile
      without growing older
      without getting colder
      without slowing my stride
      without losing my pride
      without dimming my smile.
So stop the world, for a little while.

1969

WHO and WHAT

i feel sad when i am ignored, rejected, disappointed.
i feel angry when i am disrespected and treated unjustly.
i feel impotent when i can't erase the wrongs.

i feel happiest when i am with my favorite people.
i feel creative when i am writing poetry.
i feel smart when i figure out something or realize a new thought.

i feel significant when i can make a positive change on the world.
i feel satisfied when i can comfort another person or creature.
i feel content when others respond to me as i wish them to.

I am what I feel and think,
I am what I say and do,
I am my effect on those around me and
          on the rest of the planet.

2003

ALONE

I am alone with my secrets,
with my pain, with my fears.

They burden me and darken my path. I cannot elude them.
I am alone in the company of others,
alone with my thoughts.

We are born alone and die alone; we are alone in life
despite artificial connections with others.
Talking, listening, seeing, touching, even making love . . .
none erase the sole, stark truth of alone-ness.

A solitary journey, racing toward death from the moment of birth.
We set goals, make appointments, create projects, and mark deadlines.
All fake.
The only true deadline is death, the one reservation we cannot cancel,
although medical efforts sometimes let us reschedule.

Some die young—a shorter trip;
others mature, age, and crumble on lengthier voyages.
The ill struggle to delay death; others call it forth with suicide.
Life is a book we borrow from the library and think we can keep.

Together in Heaven? Not any more so than in life.
Get comfortable with yourself. Find inner peace.
You and now are all you have.

2013

SCAVENGER HUNT

seeking, searching,
under, over, inside, outside, within, about,
never finding, never pleasing, never perching,
floating, bobbing.
looking for peace, contentment, rest, refreshment,
satisfaction, solutions,
pleasure, resolutions,
have the questions, need the answers,
yearning for tranquil, aching for serene,
seeking renewal.
dreaming of a day of inner sunshine, despite the weather,
a reason to smile from my soul.

wonder why not here for me;
looking for a long time; getting tired.

Tricky Ricki, Columbus, Ohio

It was Finals Week in my senior year at Ohio State University in Columbus, Ohio. Baker Hall, our girls' dorm, was alive with students "pulling all nighters" and complaining about how hungry they were. Some of them were studying in small groups, while others were sequestered alone with only textbooks, notes, cigarettes, and coffee for company. Radio music blared as another traditional study aid.

Being pro-active, my roommate and I considered calling the local pizza place for delivery of a few pepperoni specials, but we knew it was way after hours. We took a quick tally of the remains of everybody's care packages from home; bad news there, too. The beef jerky, envelopes of soup mix, and tins of wonderful butter cookies were gone; only a few cans of uninteresting tuna fish were left. We knew we had to take radical action. First, we collected some money from the group. Then, we climbed out of our 2nd floor window, with the help of two bed sheets knotted into a makeshift ladder, and walked three very dark blocks to a 24-hour hamburger joint on High Street.

At 2:00 a.m., Charberts was rocking with bright lights, mournful guitar music, unwashed hippies, and strong smells of tobacco and pot. We bought a dozen steaming cheeseburgers, bags of French fries, and huge cups of Coke, and walked the three seemingly even more sinister blocks back to the dorm.

Getting out was one thing, but getting back in was another. We had to negotiate our booty and we prayed we could avoid the night watchman who patrolled the building with his hourly walks around it. Meeting him would mean severe consequences, possibly expulsion from college. My roommate was only a junior, but I was a senior and had a lot to lose by taking this risk; truthfully, I had not even thought about the possibility of the failure of this caper.

Keeping vigil at the window and seeing our difficulty in climbing back up, [*shades of Rapunzel,*] our friends inside threw down a large, white, metal, bathroom garbage can for us to stand on, enabling us to reach the life-saving bed sheet.

Amazingly enough, we succeeded in our mission and were hailed as conquering heroes when we presented the longed-for food to our ravenous dorm-mates. Burgers, fries, and Cokes had never tasted as good as they did that night. Re-energized, we willingly returned to our books to finish preparing for the next day's final exams.

From this episode emerged my new nickname, Tricky Ricki. The "tricky" eventually disappeared, but "Ricki" remained.

My Own Voice

The night I heard my own voice, for the first time,
speak louder than anyone else's voice,
was when I grew up.

That night, my voice demanded
that I listen to it and heed it.
I feared failure, I feared disappointment, I feared danger,
although none of them had shapes or sizes or colors.
I feared fear, and that was the worst one of all.

When I first decided to listen to myself, instead of to others,
I felt like I was standing on a cliff, very near the edge,
light enough for the wind to carry me off like a feather.
I could feel the cool wind come close
and whisper its kiss on my cheek,
like an omen that it was around,
and that I shouldn't feel too safe.
I couldn't reason with that wind,
so I visualized it on the ground before me
and stepped on it fiercely,
stamping it out like a cigarette.

To my amazement, it worked,
and before the wind could return,
I moved in the direction of my own voice,
even stronger now,
and we walked together to safety.

RITA FIDLER DORN

WORDS ON WORDS

"A poem is a flower in an instant of eternity."
*— **Lawrence Ferlinghetti***

"Poetry is when an emotion has found its thought
and the thought has found words."
*— **Robert Frost***

POETRY FILLS MY SOUL

Poetry fills my soul,
makes me feel whole;
tells me where I should be.

It's the genre I write,
to express my insight
for all eternity.

My passion, my calling,
it keeps me from falling—
yes, that's really true.

From down here on earth,
toward Heaven with mirth,
I hope it does all that for you too.

2012

WORD STUFF

Homonyms, puns, and clever word play
are verbal high spots, any day.
Present, past, and perfect are my favored tenses,
but punctuation errors offend my senses.
Misspelled words assault my eyes,
while illegal apostrophes are no surprise.
A comma placed where it doesn't belong
motivates me to right that wrong.
And *double entendres* still delight
me on a conversational night.

– – – –

Would you patronize an antique shop called *Past Tense*?
An editing firm known as *Semantic Makeovers*?
A tile and carpet store named *Floor Play*?

– – – –

THE CURE

I have a cold, am feeling crummy;
throat is sore and nose is runny.
Refueling on chicken soup and vitamin C,
healthier tomorrow I plan to be.
Crumpled tissues high and low;
bottle of cough meds wherever I go.
Although I'm still a little heady,
by writing this poem, I feel better already.

THE ONLY PARTS THAT COUNT

Poetry is icing on cake,
rattle of snake,
      smooth of a firehouse pole;
glow of a space star,
roar of a race car
      on the way to that goal.

Cold of a snowflake,
splash in a rowboat lake,
      germs that make you sicker;
tears at a wake,
scratch of a rake,
      candle's potent flicker.

Wet of a swim,
giving in to a whim,
      headlong heft of success;
juice of a mango,
dip of a tango,
      adrenaline pumping under stress.

Poetry is connection or link,
new ways to think,
      roads to reveal deep feeling;
a smile and a wink,
being poised on the brink,
      vibes that encourage healing.

Thoughts put in order,
respecting each border,
      joy at sounds that are fun;
words in their places,
in all the right spaces—
      the sigh breathed when it's done!

2013

Printed in the United States
By Bookmasters